101
ESSENTIAL TIPS

Cooking with
CHICKEN

ESSENTIAL TIPS

Cooking with

CHICKEN

Anne Willan

A DK PUBLISHING BOOK

Editor Alexa Stace
Art Editor Ann Burnham
DTP Designer Mark Bracey
Series Editor Charlotte Davies
Series Art Editor Clive Hayball
Production Controller Lauren Britton
US Editor Laaren Brown

First American Edition, 1996
2 4 6 8 10 9 7 5 3 1

Published in the United States by DK Publishing, Inc.,
95 Madison Avenue, New York, New York 10016
Copyright © 1996 Dorling Kindersley Limited, London

ISBN 07894-05636

Text film output by The Right Type, Great Britain
Reproduced by Colourscan, Singapore
Printed and bound by Graphicom, Italy

E S S E N T I A L   T I P S

CHICKEN KNOW-HOW

1 CHOOSING CHICKEN

A wide variety of chicken is now available, both fresh and frozen. The skin should be unblemished and moist, and the breast meat should be plump. Free-range chickens are more expensive, but have a superior flavor and texture. They can usually be identified by a generous layer of fat under the skin.

The skin of the chicken should be light colored and moist

Breast meat should be plump and, on a young bird, the point of the breastbone will be flexible

2 STORING CHICKEN

Almost all chickens are sold plucked and cleaned, with their innards removed. The giblets (neck, gizzard, heart, and liver) are sometimes wrapped separately and stored in the cavity, so be sure to remove them – they can be used to make stock or gravy. A cleaned fresh chicken, giblets removed, can be kept in the refrigerator for two days or until the use-by date. Discard wrappings, place the chicken on a large dish and cover loosely. Defrost frozen chicken in the refrigerator, but do not keep for longer than two days. Store cooked chicken in the refrigerator and use within three days.

3 TYPES OF CHICKEN

Cornish game hens and poussins ("baby chickens") weigh about 1 lb (500 g). Roasting chickens weighing over 3 lb (1.4 kg) are more mature birds. Soup fowls are older, tougher birds that are best served braised or poached. Free-range chickens come in all sizes – large roasting chickens weighing up to 10 lb (4.5 kg) are sometimes available.

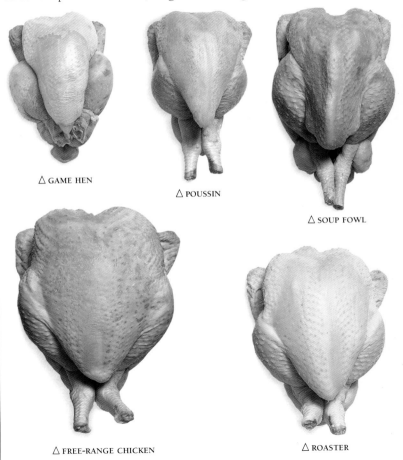

△ GAME HEN

△ POUSSIN

△ SOUP FOWL

△ FREE-RANGE CHICKEN

△ ROASTER

4 CLEANING & HANDLING

Thoroughly rinse chicken cavity before cooking, and wipe dry with paper towels. If the chicken has been frozen, blot the skin with paper towels to absorb as much moisture as possible. Wash your hands before and after handling raw chicken, and wash kitchen equipment after use.

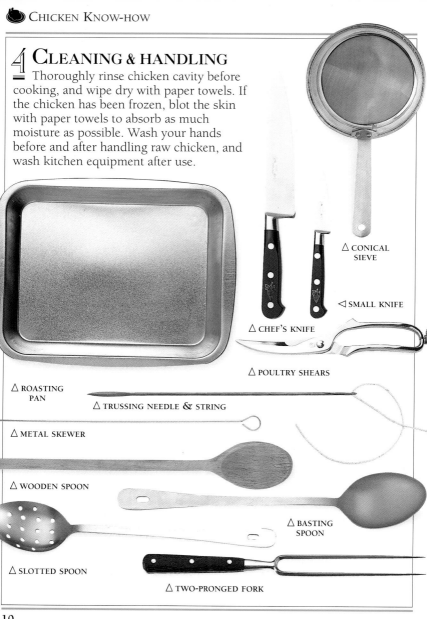

△ CONICAL SIEVE

◁ SMALL KNIFE

△ CHEF'S KNIFE

△ POULTRY SHEARS

△ ROASTING PAN

△ TRUSSING NEEDLE & STRING

△ METAL SKEWER

△ WOODEN SPOON

△ BASTING SPOON

△ SLOTTED SPOON

△ TWO-PRONGED FORK

5 FREEZING

Wrap giblets separately before freezing raw birds. Cooked chicken tends to dry out after two weeks, but in sauce or poaching liquid it will freeze for up to three months.

USE FREEZER WRAP, THEN FOIL

6 THAWING

Thaw frozen chicken in the refrigerator, allowing 3 hours per 1 lb (500 g). To speed thawing time, place the bird in its plastic wrapping in a large bowl and cover with cold water. Change the water frequently until the chicken thaws. A large bird will thaw in 3–5 hours. Cook a frozen chicken within 12 hours of thawing.

7 SERVING SIZES

These servings are approximate, depending on the recipe. Game hens and other small birds serve one. Frying or grilling chickens under 3 lb (1.4 kg) serve two to four people. Whole roasters over 3 lb (1.4 kg) serve four to six people. Mature fowls weighing more than 5 lb (2.3 kg) serve six to eight people. Large birds, weighing up to 10 lb (4.5 kg), will serve 10 to 12 people.

SERVE EVERYONE WITH BOTH WHITE & DARK MEAT

8 SALMONELLA

Poultry is highly susceptible to contamination by salmonella bacteria, causing food poisoning, so prepare, cook and store carefully.
- Raw chicken should be stored in the refrigerator for no more than two days, or until its use-by date.
- Allow frozen chicken to thaw completely before starting to cook.
- Bring a chilled chicken to room temperature before cooking.
- Wash your hands thoroughly before and after handling chicken.
- Stuff the cavity loosely.
- Cook chicken until the juices run clear when it is tested with a fork.

PREPARATION

9 PLANNING AHEAD

When cutting up a chicken, the number of pieces depends very much on the weight of the bird. A small bird, such as a game hen, can be cut in half before or after cooking. Birds that weigh 2½–3½ lb (1.2–1.6 kg) can be cut into four pieces. Birds weighing 3–5 lb (1.4–2.3 kg) can be cut into six or eight pieces. Dark meat cooks more slowly than white, so the legs should be cut into smaller pieces than the breast meat. (*See p.10 for advice on how to handle raw chicken safely.*)

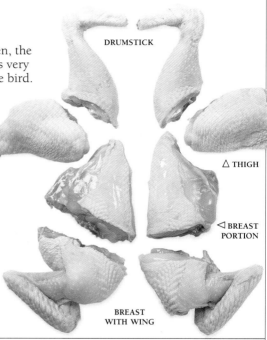

DRUMSTICK

△ THIGH

◁ BREAST PORTION

BREAST WITH WING

10 REMOVING A TENDON

The white stringlike tendons must be removed to make the flesh tender. To strip the tendon from the center of the breast, stroke it with a boning knife. If the inner fillet becomes detached, put it back. Pull off any skin and discard.

DETACH WITH A BONING KNIFE

11 CUTTING UP

You can ask the butcher to cut up a chicken for you, but the backbone may be included. To cut up a chicken, place it on a board, breast side up. Work with a sharp, heavy chef's knife, though you can also use poultry shears if preferred. Shears are especially good for splitting the breastbone, cutting out the backbone, and cutting the breast and legs in half.

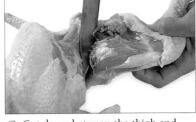

1 Cut down between the thigh and body. Sharply twist the bone outward to break the joint, then cut through it and pull the leg away.

2 Slit closely along both sides of the breastbone to loosen the flesh, then split the breastbone. Now cut along one side of the backbone to halve the bird.

3 Cut the backbone and rib bones in one piece from the breast where they are still attached, leaving the wing joints attached to the breast.

4 Cut each breast in half diagonally, cutting through the breast and rib bones so that a portion of breast meat is cut off with the wing.

5 Cut each leg in half through the joint, between the thigh and drumstick, using the line of fat as a guide. Trim off any sharp bones and fat.

12 BONING A CHICKEN

Chickens can be boned completely, for stuffing and rolling (*see p.59*), or partially, leaving the leg and wing bones to give shape, and to make carving easy. Below, partial boning is shown.

1 With a boning knife, cut the wing to leave the largest bone. Lay the bird breast down and slit the skin along the backbone. Cut out the wishbone. Cut and pull the flesh and skin away from the carcass with short, even strokes.

2 Cut the flesh from the bone near the wing and free the wing. Sever the ball and socket joints connecting the thighs to the carcass, so that they are separated from the carcass but still attached to the skin.

3 Cut the breast meat away from the bone until you reach the ridge of the breastbone, where skin and bones meet. Repeat on the other side so the skin clings only along the breastbone ridge.

4 Pull gently to separate the breastbone and carcass from the flesh – the skin tears easily. The partially boned bird, with leg and wing bones left in, is now ready for stuffing.

13 COMPLETE BONING

Larger birds weighing 3 lb (1.4 kg) or more can be boned completely, and stuffed to make a galantine or ballotine (*see p.59*). Choose a bird with the skin intact, so that you can keep it whole for wrapping and stuffing. Using a boning knife, first follow the instructions for partially boning a chicken (*see opposite*).

1 Holding the outside of the wing bone, cut through the tendons. Scrape the meat from the bone and pull it out.

2 Holding the inside end of the leg bone, cut through the tendons. Scrape the meat from the bone and cut the bone free of the skin. Remove sinews.

3 Repeat on the other side, then push the leg and wing skin side out. The bird is now completely boned. Most of the skin will have meat attached to it.

14 BONING BREASTS

Sometimes chicken breasts are sold in pairs, still joined along the breastbone in one piece; or they may be single breasts, split along the breastbone. For a double breast, place skin side up on a board. Crack down sharply with the heel of the hand to snap the breastbone. Cut out the wishbone, then cut and scrape the meat from the breastbone until it is free. Turn the breast bone side up. Scrape the meat from the ribs and cut out the bones. Remove the tendon (*see p.12*). For a single breast, turn bone side up and scrape out the bones.

15 FLATTENING BREASTS

Chicken breasts can be flattened to serve as escalopes or to stuff and roll into pinwheels. First remove the tendon, then pull out the small fillet. Slicing horizontally, cut three-quarters of the way through the breast from the long side. Open up the breast and place between two sheets of waxed paper. Pound lightly with a rolling pin until of even thickness.

Pound the breast lightly with the rolling pin to an even thickness

ALTERNATIVE
A meat mallet can also be used to flatten chicken breasts. Use gently.

16 CUTTING SUPREMES

A suprême of chicken is the skinned breast, including the wing bone. It is often poached and served with a velouté sauce (*see p.69*). Suprêmes can also be gently sautéed in butter or oil, or coated in egg and breadcrumbs and pan-fried, then served with a garnish of asparagus tips, pâté de foie gras, or truffles.

1 Cut off the legs, then remove all the skin from the breast meat, using a knife if necessary. Cut out the wishbone.

2 Cut along one side of the breastbone with a sharp knife, gently easing the meat away from the bone.

3 Continue until you reach the wing. Cut through the wing joint. Scrape the wing bone clean and trim the end.

17 SKINNING

The skin of a chicken, removed in one piece, can be used as a container for stuffing. Cut off the wing tips and trim the drumsticks. Slit the skin along the backbone. Peel the skin off one side, using short strokes with a sharp knife. Pull the skin off the leg and wing. Continue up to the breastbone then repeat on the other side.

PEEL OFF THE SKIN USING SHORT STROKES

18 STUFFING GAME HENS

Game hens are delicious stuffed with a spiced rice or couscous mixture, then cooked en cocotte in a covered roasting dish (*see p.24 for Chicken en cocotte recipe*). Rinse the cavity, wipe the birds inside and out with paper towels, then pack them loosely with the stuffing. Pull the flap of breast skin over the stuffing and around the tail to enclose it. To secure the stuffing, either truss the birds with string (*see p.18*) or hold the skin in place with skewers.

Always cook poultry immediately after stuffing because the meat can spoil quickly

DO NOT OVERFILL
Spoon the stuffing lightly into each game hen. Do not pack the stuffing tightly and overfill because the couscous filling swells during cooking and may burst out, spoiling the look of the finished dish.

19 STUFFING

Larger birds are often stuffed both at the neck end and at the cavity. (*See p.26 for recipes.*) Allow half an hour extra cooking time for small stuffed birds and up to an hour extra for larger ones. Test the thigh with a skewer for doneness.

1 First cut out and discard the wishbone (*see p.21*). Pull back the neck skin of the chicken and mound the stuffing inside with your fingers.

2 Lay the chicken breast side down, and pull the flap of neck skin over the stuffing. Truss the bird to hold the stuffing in place, or use skewers.

20 TRUSSING

Trussing helps keep the stuffing in position, and also holds the chicken together so that the sprawling legs or wings do not overcook and the cooked bird has a neat shape for carving. You will need a special trussing needle (available from kitchen speciality stores) and firm fine twine.

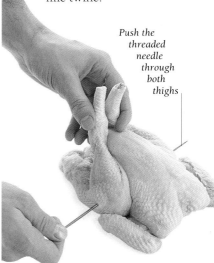

Push the threaded needle through both thighs

1 △ Lay the bird on a board, breast up, and push the legs well back and down so that the feet sit straight up in the air. Holding both feet steady with one hand, insert the threaded needle into the thigh, push through and out at the other thigh, leaving the needle still threaded.

2 △ Turn the bird over. Pull down the neck skin over the neck cavity and tuck the wing tips over. Push the needle through both sections of one wing and into the neck skin. Continue under the backbone and out through the second wing, catching both wing bones.

3 △ Turn the bird on its side. Cut the string, then pull the ends of the string firmly together and tie them securely. Turn the bird breast side up. Tuck the tail into the cavity of the chicken and fold over the top skin. Push the needle through the skin.

4 ◁ Loop the string around one drumstick, under the breastbone, and around the other drumstick. Unthread the needle and tie the ends of the string firmly together. Trim the ends of the string. The trussed chicken should now sit level on the board.

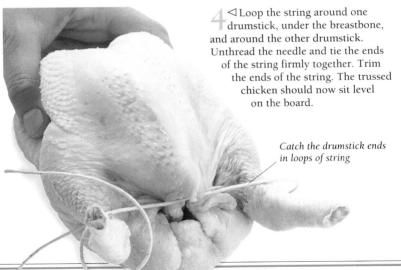

Catch the drumstick ends in loops of string

21 SPLITTING FOR GRILLING

Small birds such as game hens are often split for the grill — split, flattened, and skewered — as an attractive presentation for baking, grilling, or barbecuing. The birds can be marinated beforehand (*see p.48*) and are usually brushed with butter or oil and flavorings while cooking. Vegetables such as mushrooms, tomatoes, sliced eggplants, or zucchini can be grilled with the bird. In France, the flattened bird is often basted with herb butter while cooking.

1 First cut off the chicken's wing pinions at the joint with a pair of poultry shears, or with a sharp knife, and throw away.

2 Hold the bird in one hand, breast side down. Using poultry shears, cut along both sides of the backbone and remove it (it can be used for stock).

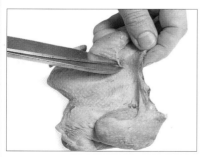

3 Using poultry shears or a sharp knife, make a small cut in the skin between the leg and breastbone on both sides and tuck in the drumsticks.

4 Thread two skewers through each bird, one through the wings and one through the legs, to hold them in a flat, splayed position while cooking.

22 REMOVING THE WISHBONE

The wishbone is sometimes removed before stuffing and roasting a chicken, making it easy to carve the breast into thin slices. Fold back the neck skin and loosen the wishbone with the point of a small knife. Remove the wishbone and any surrounding fat. Use the same technique to remove the wishbone while boning a chicken.

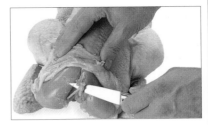

REMOVE THE BONE WITH A SMALL KNIFE

23 TESTING FOR DONENESS

It is important that the chicken is thoroughly cooked, to protect against salmonella, particularly if the chicken has previously been frozen. Test with a two-pronged fork in the thickest part of the thigh, between the leg and body – the juices from the bird should run clear and yellow, not pink. To check, lift the bird with a two-pronged fork, and tip to see the color of the juices that run out of the cavity. If there is even the slightest tinge of pink, the chicken is not yet cooked.

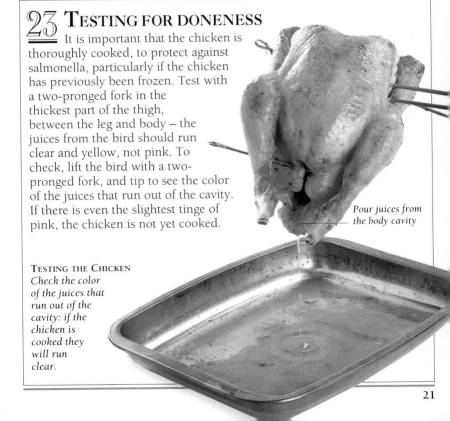

Pour juices from the body cavity

TESTING THE CHICKEN
Check the color of the juices that run out of the cavity: if the chicken is cooked they will run clear.

ROASTING

24 ROASTING METHODS

The French method of roasting poultry at a fairly high heat is the most successful. The bird tends to stew in its own juices at a lower heat. When cooking large birds, foil can be draped over the bird halfway through to keep it moist and to prevent the skin from scorching. Truss the bird (*see p.18*) and spread the skin with butter to give a golden color.

BASTE THE BIRD EVERY 10–15 MINUTES

25 ROASTING TIMES

Set the bird on its side in the roasting pan. Turn onto the other side after a quarter of the cooking time, and finally on its back so that it cooks evenly. For small birds, maintain a high heat throughout cooking. Larger birds should first be browned at a high heat, then cooked more slowly at a lower heat. Baste frequently.

Roasting times & temperatures

Size of bird	Temperature	Roasting time
Game hen	400° F/200° C	25–40 minutes total
Small chicken under 3 lb (1.4 kg)	400° F/200° C	15 minutes per 1 lb (500 g) + 15 minutes
Medium chicken, 3–5 lb (1.4–2.3 kg)	400° F/200° C	18 minutes per 1 lb (500 g) + 18 minutes
Large chicken weighing up to 10 lb (4.5 kg)	375° F/190° C	25 minutes per 1 lb (500 g)

26 SPIT-ROASTING

When birds are roasted on a turning spit, the principles are the same as for oven roasting, but the smaller the bird, the closer it should be to the heat. Make sure the bird is balanced evenly on the spit. Little or no basting is needed, since the bird cooks in its own juices as it turns, but it can be brushed with butter if preferred.

27 CLASSIC ROAST CHICKEN

Serves 4–6

Ingredients

4–4½ lb (2 kg) chicken
salt and pepper
2 large sprigs thyme
2 large sprigs rosemary
1 bay leaf
5 tbsp (75 g) butter
2 cups (500 ml) stock

TO SERVE
Potatoes roasted in oil and butter make an ideal accompaniment.

1 Preheat the oven to 425° F/220° C. Rinse chicken cavity and wipe dry with paper towels. Remove the wishbone (*see p.21*), season the chicken, and place the herbs inside.
2 Truss or skewer the chicken (*see p.18*) and place in a roasting pan that will just hold it. Slice the butter and lay over the breast.
3 Roast for 1¼–1½ hours, basting with the juices every 10–15 minutes. Turn the chicken on its breast when it starts to brown, and turn it breast up again for the last 15 minutes. Transfer to a board. Keep warm while making gravy (*see p.27*).

Frequent basting is the key to nicely browned crisp skin

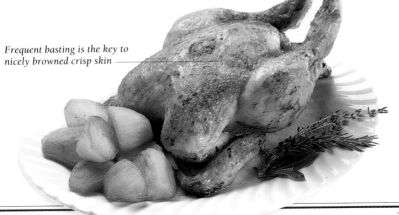

28 POT-ROASTING

Pot-roasting means cooking in the oven in a covered casserole, which should contain the bird and vegetables without crowding. Often the bird is left whole and browned first in butter before roasting.

29 CHICKEN EN COCOTTE

Serves 4

Ingredients
2 x 2 lb (1 kg) chickens
salt and pepper
zest of 2 lemons
3 tbsp butter

To Serve
Serve with cheese sauce and stir-fried vegetables.

1 Rinse the insides of the chickens, dry with paper towels and season. Remove wishbones (*see p.21*) and truss the chickens (*see p.18*).
2 Preheat the oven to 375° F/190° C. Melt the butter in a flameproof casserole, add one chicken and brown on all sides, 5–10 minutes. Remove and brown the second chicken.
3 Return the chickens to the casserole, add lemon zest and cover. Cook in preheated oven, turning occasionally so that they cook evenly.
4 After 30–40 minutes lift out the birds with a two-pronged fork. The juices from the cavity should run clear, not pink. Transfer to a board, cover with foil, and keep warm.
5 To serve, discard trussing strings and cut the chickens in half with poultry shears.

CHEESE SAUCE
For instructions on how to make the sauce see p.68.

30 STUFFED GAME HENS
Serves 4

Ingredients
4 game hens
2 tbsp butter
1 tbsp vegetable oil
salt and pepper
Stuffing
½ cup (60 g) flaked almonds
1 cup (250 ml) water
5½ oz (165 g) couscous
2 tbsp butter
Sauce
½ cup (125 ml) port
8 oz (250 g) seedless grapes
1 cup (250 ml) stock
2 tsp cornstarch
2 tbsp water
4 tbsp heavy cream

1 Preheat the oven to 375° F/190° C.
To make the stuffing, toast the almonds until browned. Boil the water, pour over the couscous and let stand for 2 minutes. Dice the butter and fork into the couscous with the toasted almonds. Season, and allow to cool.
2 Rinse the game hens, wipe with paper towels, and fill loosely with the stuffing. Pull the skin flap over and truss to secure (see p.18).
3 Heat the butter and oil in a flameproof casserole. Brown the game hens and season. Cover and cook in the oven until very tender, 50–60 minutes. Test by pricking the thickest part of the thigh; the juices should run clear. Transfer to a serving dish, cover with foil and keep warm.
4 To make the sauce, reduce the port over high heat to half. Add grapes, simmer for 1 minute, then remove. Skim fat from casserole, add stock, and boil to reduce. Strain into the port and bring to the boil. Mix cornstarch and water and whisk into port. Stir cream and grapes into sauce and reheat. Serve game hens with sauce and grapes.

TO SERVE
Scoop couscous stuffing onto plate.

31 STUFFINGS FOR CHICKEN

A seasoned stuffing not only adds flavor, but helps to plump the bird into an appealing shape. Allow about ½ cup (175 g) stuffing per 1 lb (500 g), filling the tail cavity loosely to allow the stuffing to swell while cooking. Larger birds may have another stuffing added at the neck. Stuffing must be allowed to cool before being used.

32 CHESTNUT STUFFING

Boil and peel 2 lb (1 kg) fresh chestnuts or drain a 1 lb (500 g) can of whole chestnuts in water. Coarsely crumble the chestnuts. Fry 2 chopped onions in 2 tbsp butter until soft but not brown. Stir in 1 lb (500 g) sausage meat and fry, stirring, until crumbly and brown, 5–8 minutes. Stir the sausage meat mixture into the chestnuts with 2 cups (125 g)

FRESH CHESTNUTS

fresh white breadcrumbs and ½ tsp each ground allspice and nutmeg. Season to taste. Allow to cool before using.

33 APPLE & ONION STUFFING

Gently fry 2 chopped onions with salt and pepper in 3 tbsp butter until soft but not brown. Let it cool, then stir in 1½ cups (100 g) fresh white breadcrumbs, 2 peeled, cored, and chopped tart apples, and 2 tbsp chopped fresh parsley. Add 1 beaten egg and ½ cup (125 ml) chicken stock. Season to taste.

APPLE

34 SAGE & ONION STUFFING

Gently fry 4 chopped onions in 3 tbsp butter until soft but not browned. Let it cool, then stir in 1½ cups (100 g) fresh white breadcrumbs, 3 tbsp coarsely chopped fresh sage or 1½ tbsp crumbled dried sage. Stir in 1 beaten egg and ½ cup (125 ml) chicken stock. Season to taste.

SAGE

35 HOW TO CARVE CHICKEN

To make the chicken easier to carve, remove from the roasting pan or casserole and let stand on a carving platter in a warm place for 10 minutes. When carving, give each person some white and dark meat, slicing meat from the thigh if necessary to serve everyone. Make sure you use a sharp chef's knife or carving knife, so that the breast can be cut in neat slices.

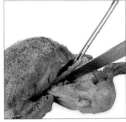

1 Cut down between leg and breast. Turn the bird on its side and cut around the oyster meat so it is attached to the thigh.

2 Spear the leg at the thigh, twist it sharply outward to break the joint, then cut through and pull the leg away.

3 Cut horizontally above the wing joint through to the breastbone, so you can carve a complete slice, then slice the breast.

36 MAKING GRAVY

Roasting a chicken in butter (see p.23) makes the basis for a rich gravy. Remove the chicken from the roasting pan and add 2 cups (500 ml) chicken stock to the cooking juices in the pan. Bring to a boil, stirring to dissolve the browned residue in the bottom of the tin. Continue boiling until the gravy is reduced and concentrated. Taste for seasoning, then strain the gravy carefully through a conical sieve into a gravy boat.

Use a conical sieve for the gravy

CAREFULLY STRAIN THE GRAVY

BRAISING & STEWING

37 BRAISING

To braise or sauté chicken, the pieces are first browned, then moistened with wine and stock.

Garlic, herbs, butter, and oil are added for flavor, while aromatic vegetables, such as shallot or leek, permeate the flesh.

38 SAUTE OF CHICKEN WITH BEER

Serves 4

Ingredients

3½ lb (1.5 kg) chicken pieces
½ cup (60 g) seasoned flour
1 tbsp vegetable oil
1 tbsp butter
2 onions, chopped
4 tbsp gin
1 cup (250 ml) dark beer
salt and pepper
4 tbsp sour cream
chopped parsley, to garnish

1 Coat the chicken with the seasoned flour. Heat the oil and butter over moderate heat. Add the chicken legs and sauté until they begin to brown, about 5 minutes. Add the breasts and cook gently until brown, 10–15 minutes.

2 Push the chicken to one side of the pan and add the onion to the other. Sauté the onion until soft but not brown, about 3 minutes. Add the gin and heat, then light carefully to flame it.

3 Spread out the chicken, season, and add half the beer. Cover and cook until the chicken is tender, 15–25 minutes. Remove the chicken from the pan and keep warm.

4 Boil sauce until reduced, add remaining beer and bring to the boil. Add chicken and heat through gently. Stir in sour cream and sprinkle with parsley.

TO SERVE
Serve with flageolet beans tossed in butter.

39 COQ AU VIN
Serves 4–6

Ingredients

4½ lb (2 kg) chicken pieces
1 tbsp vegetable oil
1 tbsp butter
4 oz (125 g) diced bacon
20 baby onions, blanched
8 oz (250 g) mushrooms
3 tbsp flour
2 cups (500 ml) chicken stock
1 garlic clove, chopped
2 shallots, chopped
1 bouquet garni
salt and pepper
Marinade
1 onion, thinly sliced
1 celery stick, thinly sliced
1 carrot, thinly sliced
1 garlic clove
6 black peppercorns
1½ cups (375 ml) red wine
2 tbsp olive oil

1 Simmer onion, celery, carrot, garlic, peppercorns, and wine for 5 minutes. Cool, then pour over chicken in a bowl. Spoon on olive oil. Cover and leave in refrigerator for 12–18 hours.
2 Strain marinade, pat chicken dry and reserve vegetables. Heat oil and butter in a flameproof casserole. Fry bacon until crisp, then remove. In turn, brown the chicken pieces and onions, then remove. Cook the mushrooms, then remove.
3 Discard all but 2 tbsp of the fat. Add marinade vegetables and cook over low heat until soft. Sprinkle with flour and brown for 2–3 minutes. Add stock, marinade, garlic, shallots, bouquet garni, salt, and pepper. Add chicken pieces and simmer until tender. Remove and keep warm.
4 Strain sauce. Add onions to sauce and cook until tender. Add mushrooms and simmer until sauce has reduced and thickened. Add chicken and bacon and reheat for 3–4 minutes.

TO SERVE
Serve with steamed potatoes.

29

40 SAUTE OF CHICKEN WITH PAPRIKA
Serves 4

Ingredients
3½ lb (1.5 kg) chicken pieces
3 tbsp paprika
salt and pepper
1 tbsp vegetable oil
1 tbsp butter
1 onion, chopped
1 cup (250 ml) stock
4 red peppers
1 tbsp tomato paste
½ cup (125 ml) sour cream

1 Sprinkle the chicken with paprika, salt, and pepper to coat evenly.
2 Heat oil and butter over moderate heat and sauté the chicken legs until they begin to brown, about 5 minutes. Add the breasts and continue cooking gently until chicken is browned on all sides. Do not let paprika scorch.
3 Push chicken to one side, add onion and cook until soft but not brown. Spread out chicken and add half the stock. Cover and cook until chicken is tender, 15–25 minutes. Remove pieces as they are cooked, testing with a fork to see if the juices run clear.
4 Meanwhile, grill the peppers, peel, then seed and slice into strips.
5 Remove all chicken pieces and keep warm. Boil pan juices down to a shiny glaze, stirring. Add

TO SERVE
White and green noodles make a cool contrast to the pungent paprika sauce.

tomato paste and remaining stock and stir until boiling.
6 Reduce the heat, return chicken to the pan, add pepper strips to the sauce and heat through gently for 1–2 minutes.
7 Add most of the sour cream and shake pan gently to mix it into sauce. Do not bring the sauce back to a boil or it will curdle. Taste for seasoning.
8 Arrange chicken and paprika sauce on plates and spoon on a little of the remaining sour cream.

41 SAUTE OF CHICKEN WITH GARLIC
Serves 4

Ingredients
3½ lb (1.5 kg) chicken pieces
salt and pepper
1 tbsp vegetable oil
6 tbsp (90 g) butter
15 garlic cloves
1 cup (250 ml) wine vinegar
1 tbsp tomato paste
2 tomatoes
1 bouquet garni
1 cup (250 ml) chicken stock

TO SERVE
*Serve with the traditional
sautéed potatoes.*

1 Season the chicken. Heat the oil and 1 tbsp of butter, add the chicken legs and brown for 5 minutes. Add the breasts and cook gently until very brown on all sides, about 10–15 minutes. Add unpeeled garlic, shake pan to distribute cloves evenly, cover, and cook over low heat for 20 minutes.

2 Stir in vinegar and simmer uncovered until reduced by half. Add tomato paste and stir into the juices. Chop tomatoes and add to pan with bouquet garni. Cover and simmer until chicken is tender and juices run clear when tested with a fork. Remove pieces as they cook and keep warm.

3 Add stock to pan and boil, stirring, until it is well reduced and concentrated in flavor. Strain sauce into another pan, and press garlic pulp through sieve with a ladle. Bring to a boil, then remove from heat. Whisk in remaining butter, piece by piece, over low heat. Taste for seasoning and serve.

42 SZECHUAN PEPPER CHICKEN
Serves 4

Ingredients
2 tbsp Szechuan peppercorns
3½ lb (1.5 kg) chicken pieces
1 tbsp vegetable oil
1 tbsp butter
1 onion, chopped
1 cup (250 ml) chicken stock
½ cup (125 ml) heavy
cream

Crush the pepper with a rolling pin

TO SERVE
Serve with a mixture of wild rice and white rice.

1 Toast the peppercorns in a small pan over very low heat, shaking the pan until they smell aromatic, 3–5 minutes. Put the peppercorns in a plastic bag and crush finely with a rolling pin.
2 Coat the chicken pieces with the crushed pepper, patting to cover the pieces evenly.
3 Heat the oil and butter in a sauté pan over moderate heat. Add the chicken legs and sauté until they begin to brown, about 5 minutes. Add the breasts and continue cooking until browned on all sides.
4 Push the chicken to one side of the pan and add the onion. Cook gently until soft but not brown, about 3 minutes.
5 Spread out the chicken in the pan again and add half the stock. Cover and cook until the chicken is tender, 15–25 minutes.
6 Remove the chicken from the pan and keep warm. Boil the pan juices until reduced to a shiny glaze. Add the remaining stock and bring back to a boil. Return the chicken to the pan and heat through gently. Add the cream to the pan and heat, stirring, until the sauce is slightly thickened.

43 STEWING

Chicken stew can be cooked on top of the stove or in the oven. The bird is cut up so that the liquid covers it completely. Slow-cooking vegetables, such as turnips and carrots, or fruit like dried prunes or apricots, can be included.

44 BRUNSWICK STEW

Serves 4–6

Ingredients

3½ lb (1.5 kg) chicken pieces
1 lb (500 g) bacon
1 tbsp brown sugar
1 bouquet garni
1 onion, chopped
3 celery sticks, thinly sliced
2 large tomatoes, skinned, seeded and diced
2 cups (250 g) shelled fava beans
1½ cups (200 g) corn
2 medium potatoes
1 tsp dried chili flakes
salt and pepper

TO SERVE
The stew needs only bread as an accompaniment.

1 Place the chicken in a casserole with the bacon and pour in water to cover. Add sugar and bouquet garni. Bring to a boil, skimming, then cover and simmer until the chicken is almost tender, 1 hour.
2 Remove the chicken with a slotted spoon and reserve. Bring the liquid back to a boil and add the onion, celery, tomatoes, and beans. Simmer, stirring frequently, until the beans are almost tender, 20–30 minutes. Add the corn and simmer for 10 minutes.
3 Meanwhile, boil the potatoes, drain, then mash finely.
4 Stir the mashed potatoes and chili flakes into the stew and season. Return the chicken and simmer until tender, 15 minutes.
5 Remove the bacon and pull the meat from the bones. Discard fat and skin and shred the meat with 2 forks. Stir the bacon into the stew, adding more water if it looks sticky. Adjust the seasoning.

45 POACHING

Poaching is an excellent method of cooking mature birds as it tenderizes them, and the juices yield a superior sauce. The vegetables are usually cooked with the bird, and all recipes are related to the classic *Poule au Pot*. Other vegetables, such as cabbage or mushrooms, may be added. The poaching liquid can be used for sauces, soup, or stock.

46 POULE AU POT
Serves 8

Ingredients
6–9 lb (3–4 kg) soup fowl
1 onion, studded with
2 cloves
1 bouquet garni
1 tsp black peppercorns
1 celery stick, chopped
1 cinnamon stick
1 tbsp salt
Stuffing
4 slices dry white bread
1 cup (250 ml) milk
½ onion, chopped
1 tbsp butter
chicken liver
8 oz (250 g) smoked ham,
minced
1 garlic clove, chopped
4 tbsp chopped parsley
pinch of grated nutmeg
salt and pepper
1 beaten egg
Vegetable garnish
1½ lb (750 g) carrots, sliced
2 lb (1 kg) leeks, sliced
into lengths
1 lb (500 g) small turnips

TO SERVE
Arrange chicken on a dish with stuffing and vegetables. Serve the broth separately.

1 To make stuffing, soak bread in milk, then squeeze dry. Fry onion in butter until soft, add liver and sauté until brown but still pink inside. Chop and mix with bread, ham, garlic, parsley, nutmeg, and egg. Season.
2 Stuff and truss chicken. Place in a large pan with onion, bouquet garni, peppercorns, celery, cinnamon and salt. Add water to cover and bring to a boil, skimming. Simmer for 1 hour.
3 Add vegetables and simmer for another hour. Remove chicken and vegetables and reduce broth to flavor. Carve the chicken to serve.

47 CHICKEN WITH PRUNES
Serves 4

Ingredients
4 lb (2 kg) soup fowl, plus
liver, chopped
2 carrots, chopped
1 bouquet garni
1 onion, stuck with 2 cloves
2 garlic cloves
1 tsp peppercorns
1 cup (300 ml) white wine
6 cups (1.5 liters) stock
salt and pepper
Stuffing
1½ cups (250 g) pitted prunes
½ cup (125 g) butter
1 onion, chopped
10 slices white bread
1 bunch parsley, chopped
zest and juice of 1 lemon
½ cup (125 ml) chicken stock

1 To make the stuffing, reserve 12 large prunes and chop the rest. Heat half the butter and cook onion until soft but not brown. Add liver and brown. Crumble the bread. Put into a bowl and stir in rest of stuffing ingredients, except reserved prunes. Add remaining butter, melted.

2 Truss the chicken and place in a flameproof casserole with carrots, bouquet garni, onion, garlic, peppercorns, wine, and enough stock to cover. Season lightly. Bring to a boil, skimming, then cover and simmer over low heat for 1½ hours. Halfway through cooking, turn the chicken over to cook evenly.

3 Meanwhile, preheat oven to 375° F/190° C. Fill the reserved prunes with stuffing. Spread the remaining stuffing in a buttered baking dish and arrange stuffed prunes on top. Cover with foil and bake for 30–40 minutes.

4 When the chicken is cooked, remove from casserole, wrap in foil and keep warm. Carve and serve coated with velouté sauce, with prunes and stuffing.

VELOUTE SAUCE
*See p.69 for
instructions on
making the sauce.*

◁ **TO SERVE**
*Cut the baked stuffing
into wedges and serve
each portion with a
few stuffed prunes.*

48 STUFFED CHICKEN BREASTS
Serves 4

Ingredients
4 large chicken breasts,
skinned and boned
4 oz (125 g) goat cheese
2–3 tbsp light cream
1 bunch basil, chopped
1 bunch parsley, chopped
3 sprigs of thyme, chopped
juice of ½ lemon
salt and pepper
Tomato butter sauce
3 shallots, chopped
1 cup (250 ml) white wine
½ cup (125 g) butter, diced
1 tbsp tomato paste

*Spread filling in an
even layer on breast*

*Leave border
around filling*

1 △ Flatten breasts (*see p.16*). Mash cheese and add cream if too dry. Mix in herbs and lemon juice and season. Spread filling in center of each breast.

2 △ Lay breast fillet (*see p.16*) on top of filling along one long edge. Loosen breast from paper and roll into a cylinder, beginning with fillet end. Fold in ends of roll so that filling is sealed in. Cut 4 large pieces of foil for wrapping.

3 △ Place breasts on foil and roll up tightly, keeping foil taut. Twist ends firmly to seal. Poach in boiling water for 15 minutes, then remove and keep warm.

4 △ Season shallots and wine and boil to a syrupy glaze. Remove from heat and whisk in butter piece by piece. Place over low heat and whisk in paste.

5 △ Unwrap rolls on paper towels to absorb any water. Cut into diagonal slices ½ in (1 cm) thick. Spoon sauce on plates and arrange slices on top.

TO SERVE
Serve with cherry tomatoes and zucchini.

FRYING

49 STIR-FRYING

Use skinned and boned chicken breasts for stir-frying. Cut the breasts neatly into very thin strips, all the same size so that they cook evenly. The character of a stir-fry is dictated by the seasonings, and with chicken there is plenty of choice (*see p.48 for marinades*).

50 ORIENTAL STIR-FRIED CHICKEN

Serves 4

Ingredients

1 oz (30 g) dried Chinese mushrooms
2 chicken breasts, cut in thin strips
4 tbsp soy sauce
4 tbsp rice wine or dry sherry
2 tsp cornstarch
6 tbsp (90 ml) vegetable oil
1 medium onion, thinly sliced
4 celery sticks, thinly sliced diagonally
1 lb (500 g) broccoli, divided into florets
1 tsp sesame oil
¼ cup (45 g) sliced almonds, toasted

1 △ Soak mushrooms for 30 minutes, then drain, reserving liquid, and slice. Toss chicken with soy sauce, wine, and cornstarch. Heat half the oil in a wok and stir-fry the vegetables for 3–4 minutes.

2 ◁ Remove the vegetables when tender but crisp; keep warm. Heat the remaining oil in the wok. Drain the chicken, reserving the marinade, and stir-fry over high heat for 2–3 minutes.

Put the warm vegetables back into the wok

4 △ Pour in the reserved marinade and cook, stirring for 2 minutes until slightly thickened. Sprinkle with the sesame oil and toasted almonds.

3 △ Return the vegetables to the wok and stir until mixed. Stir in 4 tbsp of the mushroom liquid.

TO SERVE
*Chinese egg noodles
are the ideal
accompaniment
for this dish.*

FRYING

51 PAN-FRYING

Chicken can be pan-fried in butter, vegetable oil, or bacon fat, usually with a coating of seasoned flour to help retain moisture.

52 BACON-FRIED CHICKEN

Serves 4

Ingredients
3½ lb (1.6 kg) chicken pieces
2 cups (500 ml) milk
½ cup (60 g) flour seasoned
with 2 tsp pepper
8–12 bacon slices
Gravy
2 tbsp flour
1½ cups (375 ml) milk
dash of Tabasco
salt and pepper

1 Soak chicken in milk for 8–12 hours, covered. Drain, then coat the chicken lightly with flour.
2 Fry bacon in a pan until crisp and brown and fat is released. Drain on paper towels and keep warm.
3 Fry chicken in bacon fat over low heat until brown and tender. Drain on paper towels and keep warm.
4 To make gravy, brown flour in pan, add milk and whisk until thickened. Add dash of Tabasco and season. Crumble the bacon over chicken pieces and serve with the gravy.

53 SOUTHERN FRIED CHICKEN

Serves 4

Ingredients
3½ lb (1.6 kg) chicken pieces
2 cups (500 ml) milk
½ cup (60 g) flour seasoned
with 2 tsp pepper
1 cup (250 ml) vegetable oil
Gravy
2 tbsp flour
1½ cups (375 ml) milk
salt and pepper

TO SERVE
Arrange chicken on serving dish and serve the gravy separately.

1 △ Place the chicken in a bowl, pour over the milk, cover, and let soak for 8–12 hours, then drain. Spread the flour in a shallow dish and coat the chicken evenly, patting off excess.

2 △ Heat oil in a frying pan. Brown the chicken on all sides for 3–5 minutes, then reduce heat and cook until brown and tender when pierced with a fork. Remove pieces as cooked.

3 △ Transfer chicken to dish lined with paper towels and keep warm. Do not cover or coating will soften. Pour off all but 2 tbsp of fat from the pan. Sprinkle in the flour and stir until browned. Whisk in the milk and simmer until the sauce is smooth and has thickened, about 2 minutes. Season to taste and pour into a gravy boat.

54 DEEP-FRYING

The purpose of deep-frying is to seal food by immersing it in hot oil so that the flavor and juices are retained in a crisp crust. Deep-fried chicken is particularly successful, but it must have a coating to protect it from the heat. A coating of flour, egg, and breadcrumbs gives the best protection. The amount of oil is important: make sure there is at least ¾ in (2 cm) in the pan. Do not fry food that is too cold, and always add food in small batches.

55 OIL TEMPERATURE

Fry with peanut or corn oil, as they are bland and have a high smoking point. Heat the oil to 180° C (350° F) on a deep-fat thermometer, or until a cube of fresh bread turns brown in 30 seconds.

TESTING THE OIL TEMPERATURE

56 CHICKEN POJARSKI

Serves 4

Ingredients
6 individual brioches
½ cup (125 ml) milk
14 oz (425 g) chicken breasts, skinned
3 tbsp heavy cream
ground nutmeg
salt and pepper
¼ cup (30 g) seasoned flour
1 egg
oil for deep-frying

1 △ Dice 4 of the brioches and reserve. Break up the remaining brioches, place in a bowl, pour on the milk, and let soak for 5 minutes. Squeeze out any excess milk. Cut the chicken into chunks. Work the chicken and soaked brioches through the fine blade of a mincer or use a food processor, but do not purée too finely.

2 △ Using a wooden spoon, beat the cream into the minced chicken mixture with a pinch of nutmeg and seasoning. With wet hands, shape the mixture into 4 balls and flatten slightly. Coat the balls evenly in the seasoned flour, patting off any excess, then brush with beaten egg and drain.

3 △ Place the diced brioches in a bowl. Coat each chicken round in the chopped brioches, patting until they are completely covered. Chill, uncovered, for about 30 minutes, to allow the rounds to firm up. Preheat the oven to 375° F/190° C. Heat the oil in a deep-fryer to 350° F/180° C.

4 △ Deep-fry the rounds, 1–2 at a time, until they are brown, 2–3 minutes. Using a slotted spoon, transfer to a baking sheet as they are fried. Bake in the preheated oven until a skewer inserted in the center is hot to the touch, 25–30 minutes. Cover with foil if browning too quickly. Place on warmed plates and spoon sauce around.

TO SERVE
Serve with tomato sauce (see p.67) *and kasha (buckwheat).*

GRILLING & BARBECUING

57 GRILLING

Poultry should be grilled in fairly large pieces, with plenty of bone to disperse the heat. Small birds, split for grilling, grill particularly well. Marinating poultry beforehand helps, as does brushing with melted butter.

58 CHICKEN THIGHS IN YOGURT

Serves 4

Ingredients
8 chicken thighs
1 cup (250 ml) yogurt
salt and pepper
vegetable oil

1 Place chicken in a bowl with the yogurt and season. Turn the chicken until coated, then cover and let marinate in the refrigerator for 3–4 hours.

2 Heat the grill and brush the rack with oil. Remove the chicken from the marinade, scrape off the yogurt, and dry on paper towels. Arrange on the rack.

3 Grill the chicken thighs about 3 in (7 cm) from the heat until they are very brown. Turn and cook on the other side until the skin is very brown and the juices run clear when tested with a fork. Serve with tabbouleh, and cilantro sauce.

CILANTRO SAUCE
To make the sauce see instructions on p.68.

59 HOW TO FLATTEN A CHICKEN

Set the chicken breast side down and cut along both sides of the backbone. Discard the bone and trim off any flaps of skin. Open up the bird and snip out the wishbone. Turn the bird breast side up and cut off the wing tips. With the heel of your hand, and using both hands, push down sharply on the breast to break the breastbone and flatten the bird. Make a small cut in the skin between the leg and breastbone on both sides and tuck in the legs.

TO FLATTEN
Use both hands to break the breastbone of the chicken and flatten the bird.

60 DEVILED CHICKEN

Serves 4

Ingredients
3 lb (1.4 kg) chicken
2 fresh red chilies
½ cup (125 ml) lemon juice
2 tbsp olive oil
salt and pepper

1 Split and flatten the chicken (see above) and place in a large dish. Core, seed, and chop chilies and mix with lemon juice, 1 tbsp oil, and 2 tsp black pepper. Pour over the chicken, cover, and let marinate in the refrigerator for 8 hours, turning occasionally.
2 Heat the grill and brush rack with oil. Remove chicken from marinade, insert 2 skewers to hold it flat, then set on rack skin-side up and sprinkle with salt.
3 Grill 4 in (10 cm) from the heat, basting with the marinade, until the skin is golden brown, 15–20 minutes. Turn and continue grilling until the juices run clear, 20–30 minutes.

TO SERVE
Serve with grilled tomatoes with breadcrumb topping.

61 GRILLED GAME HENS
Serves 2

Ingredients
2 game hens
2 tbsp butter, melted
vegetable oil, for brushing
salt and pepper
1 tbsp Dijon mustard
¼ cup (15 g) dried
breadcrumbs

MUSHROOM SAUCE
*See p.68 for instructions on
making the sauce.*

TO SERVE
*Serve with French fries and
mushroom sauce.*

1 △ Split and flatten the game hens
(*see p.45*). Thread a skewer through
the wings to hold the hens flat, then
thread a second skewer through the
legs. Brush the hens evenly with half
the melted butter and season.

2 △ Heat the grill. Oil the grill rack,
then place the game hens on the
rack, skin side up. Grill the game hens
about 3 in (7 cm) from the heat for 15
minutes, basting them once with a little
of the remaining melted butter.

3 △ Turn the game hens with a 2-pronged fork and brush the other side with the remaining melted butter. Return to the heat and grill for 10 minutes on the other side. If the hens brown too quickly, lower the grill rack further away from the heat.

4 △ Turn the game hens again skin side up, brush with the mustard, then sprinkle with the breadcrumbs. Grill, skin side towards the heat, until the thigh is tender when pierced with a fork, about 10 minutes longer.

62 GRILLED CHICKEN WITH HERB BUTTER

Serves 4

Ingredients
3 lb (1.4 kg) chicken
1 small bunch tarragon, chopped
1 small bunch chervil, chopped
2 garlic cloves, chopped
1 tsp lemon juice
½ cup (125 g) butter, softened
salt and pepper

Flatten the chicken (see p.45). Beat herbs, garlic, and lemon juice into the butter and season. With your fingers, loosen the skin on breast and thighs and insert butter under the skin. Skewer the chicken and grill for 20 minutes skin side up, and 15 minutes skin side down. Turn again, baste with pan juices, and grill for 10–15 minutes.

TO SERVE
Cut the chicken into 4 pieces and serve garnished with fresh chervil or tarragon.

63 BARBECUED CHICKEN

Chicken wings, thighs, drumsticks, and kebabs are all popular barbecue fare, excellent cooked on a charcoal grill. Take care not to overcook; although the barbecue is ideal for drawing out the flavor, the intense heat can dry delicate meat rapidly. Marinating helps, as does brushing with melted butter or oil.

64 MARINADES

Chicken pieces or kebabs are usually marinated before being stir-fried or barbecued. The marinade tenderizes and adds flavor, and also helps protect the meat from the heat of the cooking flame. The type of oil you use – olive, sesame, peanut, or corn – and the seasonings you choose will all add character. Start with scallion, garlic, fresh ginger, and shallot, adding a touch of vinegar, lemon, or soy sauce. Try a Greek marinade of yogurt and oregano, or an Asian one of soy sauce, rice wine, and hot peppers. The chicken pieces should be skinned, to allow the flavors to penetrate the flesh, and the chicken should be left in the refrigerator to marinate for 2–3 hours.

STIR TO COAT WELL

65 BARBECUED GAME HENS

Serves 4

Ingredients
4 game hens
Marinade
1 cup (125 ml) olive oil
3 tbsp lemon juice
1 tsp crushed peppercorns
1 tsp dried chili flakes
salt

1 Split and flatten the game hens (*see p.45*). Insert skewers through wings and legs to hold them flat.
2 Whisk together the olive oil, lemon juice, peppercorns, and chili flakes. Pour over the birds and brush to coat well. Let marinate for 3 hours, turning occasionally.
3 Grill or barbecue for 25–30 minutes until brown and slightly charred, turning frequently.

66 DEVILED DRUMSTICKS
Serves 4

Ingredients
8 drumsticks
vegetable oil, for brushing
Devil mixture
2 tbsp mango chutney
½ cup (125 g) butter, melted
2 tbsp tomato paste
2 tbsp Worcestershire sauce
1 tsp ground nutmeg
½ tsp anchovy paste
salt and pepper
pinch of cayenne pepper

To Serve
Serve the drumsticks with potato salad tossed with vinaigrette.

1 First make the devil mixture. Chop up any large pieces of fruit in the chutney, then mix in a bowl with remaining ingredients.
2 Heat the grill and brush the rack with oil. Skin the drumsticks and slash each one diagonally in several places with a sharp knife.
3 Brush each drumstick with the devil mixture, working it well into the slashes. Arrange the drumsticks on the oiled rack.
4 Grill or barbecue the drumsticks 4 in (10 cm) from the heat, turning once. Baste frequently with the remaining devil mixture and any pan juices. Cook until well browned and tender, about 10–12 minutes on each side.
5 Serve the drumsticks hot or cold, with potato salad tossed with vinaigrette and chopped parsley and chives.

67 INDONESIAN KEBABS
Serves 6

Ingredients
3½ lb (1.6 kg) chicken breasts,
skinned and boned
Marinade
3 shallots, finely chopped
2 garlic cloves, finely chopped

½ tsp chili powder
2 tsp ground coriander
2 tsp ground ginger
3 tbsp soy sauce
2 tbsp wine vinegar
2 tbsp vegetable oil

TO SERVE
*Serve the kebabs
with a mixed salad
and peanut sauce.*

1 △ Cut the fillet from each chicken breast in half lengthwise, then cut each breast into thin strips of the same size. Place the remaining ingredients in a large bowl and mix well.

2 △ Add the chicken strips to the bowl and turn until they are well coated with the marinade. Cover with plastic wrap and refrigerate for at least 3 hours, or up to 12 hours.

3 ▷ Thread the chicken strips onto pre-soaked bamboo skewers, accordion fashion, 3 strips per skewer, twisted slightly. Grill the kebabs 2–3 in (5–7 cm) from the heat for 2–3 minutes until browned. Then turn and brown the other side for 2–3 minutes more.

PEANUT SAUCE
See p.69 for instructions on how to make the sauce.

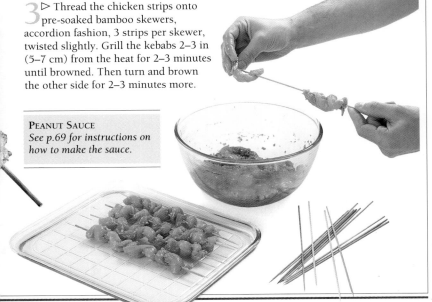

BAKING

BAKING

68 BAKING CHICKEN

Baking is an ideal way of sealing in the juices, whether the bird is cooked in a Dutch oven, earthenware tagine, or casserole, in a paper or foil parcel (*en papillote*), or encased in a pastry crust.

69 MOROCCAN CHICKEN WITH SPICES
Serves 4

Ingredients
1 lb (500 g) tomatoes
6 onions
3½ lb (1.6 kg) chicken, jointed
large pinch of saffron
2–3 sprigs parsley, chopped
½ cup (75 g) dried apricots, chopped
2 tbsp honey
2 tsp ground cinnamon
1 tsp ground ginger
salt and pepper
½ cup (125 ml) olive oil

1 Preheat oven to 350° F/180° C. Peel, seed, and chop the tomatoes. Slice 4 onions and chop the remainder finely. Place the chicken in a tagine or heavy casserole and cover with the sliced onions and tomatoes.
2 Mix the remaining ingredients together in a bowl, then spoon over the chicken in an even layer.
3 Cover tightly and bake in the preheated oven until the chicken is tender when tested with a fork, about 1½ hours.

TO SERVE
Serve with couscous and almond stuffing (see p.25).

70 CHICKEN & HAM PIE
Serves 8–10

Ingredients
1½ lb (750 g) chicken breasts,
skinned and boned
12 oz (375 g) lean ground pork
12 oz (375 g) lean ham, cubed
9 eggs, 6 hard-cooked
zest of ½ lemon
1 tsp dried thyme
1 tsp dried sage
pinch of ground nutmeg
salt and pepper
butter, for greasing
Pastry
3½ cups (500 g) flour
2 tsp salt
5 tbsp (75 g) butter
5 tbsp (75 g) lard
⅔ cup (150 ml) water

TO SERVE
Unmould pie when cold.

1 △ Make pastry in a food processor, then chill. Roll out three-quarters of the pastry ¼ in (5 mm) thick and use to line a greased, 8 in (20 cm) springform pan, leaving a ½ in (1 cm) overhang.

2 △ Preheat oven to 400° F/200° C. Cube 2 chicken breasts, grind remainder and mix both with pork and ham. Beat in 2 eggs, lemon zest, thyme, sage, nutmeg, salt, and pepper. Spread half the filling in the pan and place hard-cooked eggs on top. Cover with remaining filling and fold pastry over.

3 △ Brush pastry with beaten egg. Roll out remaining pastry for the lid and make leaves with trimmings. Lay the lid over the filling and press edges to seal. Brush with egg, add leaves, and brush again. Make a steam hole. Bake for 1 hour, then reduce heat and bake for 30 minutes. Allow to cool, then chill.

SALADS & COLD DISHES

71 BONING CHICKEN FOR COLD DISHES

To bone cooked chicken, first cut down between leg and body joints. Twist leg, cut through joint, and pull off leg. Slit along breastbone, loosen breast meat and remove each breast half in one piece. Remove wishbone.

CUT THROUGH LEG JOINT & PULL OFF

72 COBB SALAD

Serves 4–6

Ingredients

6 oz (175 g) bacon
1 lb (500 g) cooked chicken meat, boned
1 shallot, finely chopped
vinaigrette (see p.57)

½ head lettuce, shredded
2 large tomatoes, thinly sliced
3 oz (90 g) Roquefort cheese
2 avocados, peeled and sliced

1 Fry the bacon until crisp, then drain on paper towels. Crumble.
2 Toss chicken and shallot with one-third of the vinaigrette. Toss lettuce with more vinaigrette.
3 Arrange salad on plates and drizzle with remaining vinaigrette.

TO SERVE
Sprinkle the avocados with lemon juice, if necessary, to prevent discoloration.

73 CHICKEN WITH SAFFRON RICE

Serves 4–6

Ingredients

1 lb (500 g) cooked chicken
3 tbsp lemon juice
6 tbsp (90 ml) vegetable oil
½ tsp paprika
cherry tomatoes, peeled
Saffron rice
large pinch of saffron
1½ cups (300 g) rice
3 celery sticks, thinly sliced
Curry dressing
1 onion, finely chopped
6 tbsp (90 ml) vegetable oil
1 tbsp curry powder
4 tbsp tomato juice
4 tbsp wine vinegar
2 tsp apricot jam
2 tbsp lemon juice
1 cup (250 g) cottage cheese
salt and pepper

1 Bring 3 cups (750 ml) water to a boil with saffron and pinch of salt. Simmer for 2 minutes. Stir in rice and bring back to a boil. Cover and simmer until tender, 15–20 minutes.

2 To make dressing, sauté the onion in 1 tbsp oil until soft but not brown. Add curry powder and stir gently for 2 minutes. Add tomato juice and vinegar and simmer until reduced by half. Stir in the jam, then cool.

3 Blend the dressing in a food processor until smooth, then blend in the lemon juice and cheese. Add the remaining oil slowly. Season.

4 Shred the chicken and toss with half the curry dressing. Make a vinaigrette with the lemon juice and oil, add to the rice with the celery, and toss with 2 forks to combine.

5 Pile rice salad on a platter and arrange chicken on top. Sprinkle with paprika.

TO SERVE
Garnish with peeled cherry tomatoes.

74 CHICKEN MOUSSE
Serves 4

Ingredients
1 lb (500 g) chicken breasts
2 egg whites
salt and pepper
pinch of ground nutmeg
¾ cup (175 ml) heavy cream
2 zucchini, thinly sliced
melted butter for greasing

TO SERVE ▷
*Serve with toast
and madeira sauce*
(see p.67).

1 △ Grind the chicken finely, then place in a bowl set over a large bowl of iced water. Whisk the egg whites, then gradually mix into the chicken. Season and add nutmeg. Beat in the cream gradually and chill until firm.

2 △ Blanch the zucchini slices and drain. Butter 6 ramekins and line the bottoms with circles of baking parchment. Brush with melted butter. Line the ramekins with overlapping circles of zucchini slices.

3 △ Preheat oven to 350° F/180° C.
Spoon the chicken mixture into the
ramekins and smooth the tops. Place
the ramekins in a baking dish and pour
in boiling water to come more than
halfway up the sides. Bring the water to
a boil on top of the stove.

4 △ Cover dish with baking
parchment and bake in preheated
oven until a skewer inserted into the
center is hot to the touch, 20–30
minutes. Drain off excess liquid,
unmould ramekins and allow to cool.

75 TEX-MEX SALAD
Serves 4–6

Ingredients

1 lb (500 g) cooked chicken, thinly sliced
1 shallot, finely chopped
1 large head romaine lettuce, shredded
2 large tomatoes, thinly sliced
1 red pepper, cored, seeded, and diced
1 cup (175 g) canned corn, drained
1–2 chilies, seeded and finely chopped
Vinaigrette
4 tbsp red wine vinegar
2 tsp Dijon mustard
¾ cup (175 ml) vegetable oil
salt and pepper
3 sprigs tarragon, finely chopped

1 Whisk vinegar, mustard, oil, salt,
and pepper, then stir in tarragon.
2 Toss chicken and shallot with a
third of the dressing. Toss lettuce
with another third of the dressing.
3 Arrange salad on plates, drizzle
with remaining dressing and
sprinkle with chopped chili.

TO SERVE
Tortilla chips make a crunchy contrast.

76 CHICKEN LIVERS

The liver should not be dark or strong-smelling, nor tinged with green from the gall bladder. Livers add richness to terrines, and can be used to make pâté. Be careful not to overcook, or they become dry.

77 CHICKEN LIVER SALAD

Serves 4

Ingredients

8 oz (250 g) crisp lettuce, torn
4 oz (125 g) sliced bacon, diced
5 tbsp (75 ml) vegetable oil
4 slices French bread, cubed
8 oz (250 g) chicken livers, sliced
salt and pepper
3 shallots, finely chopped
1 garlic clove, finely chopped
1 tbsp raspberry vinegar
chopped chives, to garnish

TO SERVE
Toss the salad with the hot pan juices until wilted, then sprinkle with chives.

Place lettuce in bowl. Fry bacon and add to bowl. Fry bread in oil and add to bowl. Fry livers until brown but pink inside. Add to salad and season. Cook shallots and garlic for 1 minute, add vinegar, reduce by half, then pour on salad and toss.

78 CHICKEN LIVER PATE

Rich, smooth pâtés are often liver-based and can be distinguished with unusual flavorings. Apples and brandy go well with chicken livers. However, moist ingredients must be used sparingly, or pâtés become too soft and do not keep well. Do not cook chicken livers for too long or they will become grainy.

Slice the livers, and sauté them gently in butter or oil until they are browned, but still pink inside. Purée with flavorings, such as diced apple, garlic, and brandy, or wine and shallots, season to taste, and transfer to a serving bowl or individual ramekins. Cover each one with melted butter or lard.

79 COUNTRY TERRINE

Cook terrines in an earthenware mold with a tight-fitting lid. Line the mold with pork fat, or strips of bacon. Make the mixture from 1 lb (500 g) ground pork, and 8 oz (250 g) each ground veal and ground chicken livers. Beat in a chopped onion softened in butter, a pinch each of ground allspice, nutmeg, and cloves, 2 chopped garlic cloves, 2 eggs, and 2 tbsp brandy. Spread one-third of the mixture in the terrine, add 4 oz (125 g) ham strips. Top with another third of mixture, add another 4 oz (125 g) of ham strips and remaining mixture. Cover with fat strips, a sprig of thyme, and a bay leaf. Put on lid and bake in a bain-marie in a preheated oven at 350° F/180°C for 1½ hours. Cool.

COOK THE TERRINE IN A MOLD

80 GALANTINES

A galantine is a roll made from a chicken that has been boned, the skin kept in one piece. The skin is then stuffed with a mixture made with the ground chicken meat, liver and other meats, strips of ham, chopped onion, herbs, spices, garlic, and beaten egg. The galantine is shaped into a cylinder so that it is easy to slice, then wrapped in a cloth and poached in stock. It is always served cold, usually coated in aspic.

SERVE THE GALANTINE COLD, WITH ASPIC

81 BALLOTINES

A ballotine is also made with a boned chicken, the skin stuffed with a mixture of the chicken meat, herbs, and spices. A ballotine may be rolled, or sewn into a cushion shape. It is poached or braised like a roast, to serve hot in a rich sauce made from the cooking liquid, or presented cold in aspic like a galantine.

RICE & NOODLES

82 CHICKEN CURRY
Serves 6

Ingredients
3½ lb (1.6 kg) chicken pieces
salt and pepper
4 tbsp vegetable oil
1 large eggplant, diced
1 onion, finely chopped
5 garlic cloves, chopped
2 tsp chopped fresh ginger
2 tbsp garam masala
1 tbsp plain flour
1 lb (500 g) tomatoes, chopped
1 lb (500 g) canned
chickpeas, drained

TO SERVE
Serve with saffron rice.

Season chicken.
Brown in oil in a
large casserole and
remove. Brown the
eggplant and remove.
Add onion, garlic, and ginger and cook until
soft. Stir in garam masala and flour and cook for
2 minutes. Add tomatoes, chicken, and water
and simmer for 20 minutes. Add eggplant and
chickpeas and cook until chicken is tender.

83 PAELLA
Serves 8–10

Ingredients
3 onions, chopped
2 peppers, cored, seeded, and sliced
4 tbsp olive oil
1¼ lb (650 g) short-grain rice
6 cups (1.5 liters) chicken stock
large pinch of saffron, soaked in hot water
3 garlic cloves, crushed
salt and pepper
1 lb (500 g) prepared squid, sliced
1 lb (500 g) smoked ham, cut in strips
1 lb (500 g) chorizo sausage, sliced
1½ lb (750 g) tomatoes, peeled and chopped
1 lb (500 g) cooked green peas
1 lb (500 g) chicken breast, cut in strips
1½ lb (750 g) unpeeled shrimp
3 lb (1.4 kg) mussels in their shells, scrubbed

Cook onions and peppers in oil
until soft. Add rice and stir until
transparent. Add stock, saffron,
and garlic and season. Add squid,
ham, sausage, tomatoes, peas, and
chicken in layers. Cover and cook
until rice is tender. Add shrimp
and mussels for last 10 minutes.

84 MALAY CHICKEN
Serves 6

Ingredients
6 shallots, sliced
3 garlic cloves, crushed
3 dried red chilies, seeded
1½ tsp ground turmeric
1 tbsp ground coriander
3 in (7 cm) piece fresh ginger, sliced
2 tbsp vegetable oil
1½ lb (750 g) poached chicken, cubed
2½ cups (600 ml) chicken stock
8 oz (250 g) peeled shrimp
8 oz (250 g) tofu, cubed
8 oz (250 g) bean-sprouts
4 oz (125 g) rice noodles, soaked
2 cups (500 ml) coconut milk

1 Process shallots, garlic, chilies, turmeric, coriander, and ginger to a smooth paste. Heat oil in a wok, add paste, and stir-fry for 2 minutes.
2 Add chicken and stock and simmer for 20 minutes. Add shrimp, tofu, bean-sprouts, noodles, and coconut milk. Simmer for 5 minutes.

TO SERVE
Serve sprinkled with scallions.

85 NASI GORENG
Serves 4

TO SERVE
Add more soy sauce to taste.

Ingredients
1 garlic clove, chopped
1 onion, chopped
1 tsp dried shrimp paste
1 tsp crushed chilies
3 tbsp oil
6 oz (175 g) skinned chicken breast, sliced
4 oz (125 g) large peeled shrimp
1 cup (250 g) long-grain rice, cooked
2 scallions
2 tbsp soy sauce
1 x 2-egg omelette, cut into strips

1 Blend garlic, onion, shrimp paste, and chilies. Stir-fry in 1 tbsp oil. Add chicken and shrimp. Stir-fry for 3 minutes then remove.
2 Heat remaining oil and stir-fry cold rice. Add scallions, soy sauce, omelette strips, chicken, and shrimp and stir-fry until hot.

SOUPS & STOCKS

86 CHICKEN STOCK

Chicken stock is an indispensable ingredient in sauces and soups. Place 2 lb (1 kg) raw chicken bones or a soup fowl in a pan with onion, carrot, celery, bouquet garni, and 5 peppercorns. Add enough water to cover and simmer for 3 hours, skimming. Strain and cool. Keep stock in refrigerator, covered, for up to 3 days. It also freezes well.

SKIM FAT FROM STOCK

87 MAKING CHICKEN SOUP

The simplest chicken soup consists of the stock produced by boiling or poaching a whole chicken, as in *Poule au pot* (*see p.34*). The longer the soup is simmered, the more flavor it will have. Add 4 oz (125 g) fine noodles and simmer for 5 minutes, or add slices of toasted bread to soup bowls and pour on the soup.

88 CHICKEN CONSOMME

Makes 4 cups (1 liter)

Ingredients
2 carrots, chopped
2 leeks, chopped
2 celery sticks, chopped
2 tomatoes, chopped
12 oz (375 g) chicken giblets or pieces, skinned
3 egg whites, beaten
6 cups (1.5 liters) chicken stock
salt and pepper

Mix vegetables, chicken and egg whites in a bowl. Heat the stock and season. Whisk into the bowl and return to the pan. Bring slowly to the boil, whisking for at least 10 minutes. As soon as it is frothy, stop whisking. Make a hole in the center of the crust. Simmer for 30–40 minutes then strain through a sieve lined with a damp dish towel and cool.

89 CHICKEN CONSOMMÉ WITH MADEIRA

Serves 4–6

Ingredients

2 carrots, sliced
2 celery sticks, cut in chunks
2 leeks, green parts only
1½ lb (750 g) tomatoes, peeled
3 egg whites
12 oz (375 g) chicken wings
salt and pepper
6 cups (1.5 liters) chicken stock
4 tbsp Madeira

TO SERVE

Garnish with thin tomato strips and serve with melba toast.

1 Work all the vegetables in a food processor until roughly chopped. Whisk the egg whites in a large bowl until frothy. Add the vegetables, chicken wings, salt, and pepper and stir until well mixed. Pour the cold stock into the mixture and stir well. Pour the mixture into a large pan and bring slowly to a boil, whisking constantly, about 10 minutes. When the liquid is frothy and looks white, stop whisking.

2 Lower the heat and with a ladle make a hole in the layer of vegetables on the surface so that the consommé can simmer. Simmer until the consommé is clear and a solid crust has formed on the surface. Ladle the consommé into a sieve lined with a damp dish towel and allow to drain slowly. Blot off any surface fat with paper towels. Bring consommé almost to a boil, then add the Madeira.

90 CHICKEN GUMBO

Serves 6–8

Ingredients

5 tbsp (75 ml) vegetable oil
¼ cup (30 g) flour
1 onion, finely chopped
2 garlic cloves, chopped
2 peppers, seeded and diced
1 celery stick, sliced
1 lb (500 g) okra, sliced
8 oz (250 g) tomatoes,
    peeled and chopped
2 tbsp tomato paste
1 bunch parsley, chopped
3 sprigs thyme, chopped
1 bay leaf
4 cups (1 liter) stock
¼ tsp cayenne pepper
salt and black pepper
12 chicken thighs, skinned
8 oz (250 g) ham, diced
1¼ cups (300 g) rice

1 Heat the oil in a large flameproof casserole, add flour, and stir over low heat until browned.
2 Add the onion, garlic, peppers, and celery, and stir until lightly browned, 8–10 minutes. Stir in the okra, tomatoes, tomato paste, half the herbs, the bay leaf, chicken stock, cayenne pepper, salt, and pepper and bring to a boil.
3 Add the chicken thighs, pushing them down into the mixture. Simmer, stirring occasionally, for 30 minutes. Stir in the ham and simmer until the chicken is tender, about another 30 minutes.
4 Remove from the heat. Allow to cool slightly, then remove thigh meat from the bones and shred. Return meat to casserole.
5 Boil the rice until tender and drain. Reheat gumbo and taste for seasoning. Serve hot.

TO SERVE
*Boiled rice is
the traditional
accompaniment.*

91 JAPANESE CHICKEN BROTH
Serves 4

Ingredients
2 oz (60 g) cellophane
noodles
12 oz (375 g) chicken breasts
1 carrot, sliced in thin strips
8 oz (250 g) tofu, cubed
½ Chinese cabbage, shredded
4 scallions, sliced
4 shiitake mushrooms, sliced
8 fresh clams, shelled
4 oysters, shucked
Dipping Sauce
juice of 1 lemon
3 tbsp sweet rice wine
1 tbsp rice wine
1 in (2.5 cm) dried kelp
1 tsp dried bonito flakes
5 tbsp (75 ml) soy sauce
Stock
4 cups (1 liter) water
4 in (10 cm) dried kelp
1 tsp dried bonito flakes
2 tbsp soy sauce
2 tbsp sweet rice wine

1 To make dipping sauce, combine lemon juice, rice wines, kelp, bonito, and soy sauce in a bowl. Let steep for at least 1 hour, then strain.
2 For the stock, bring water to a boil with kelp then strain, discarding kelp. Sprinkle on bonito flakes, let steep 5 minutes, then strain through cheesecloth. Add soy sauce and rice wine.
3 Soak the noodles in hot water for 30 minutes, then drain. Skin chicken and cut into thin strips.
4 Bring stock to a boil, add chicken and carrot, and cook for 2–3 minutes. Add half each of the tofu, vegetables, and noodles and cook 2–3 minutes. Add half the shellfish and cook until oysters start to curl. Serve with dipping sauce.
5 When ready, return stock to pan, add remaining ingredients and cook until tender.

TO SERVE
*Set soup over a tabletop burner so guests
can help themselves with chopsticks.*

Sauces

SAUCES

92 SAUCES FOR CHICKEN

Chicken can be served with a variety of sauces, both hot and cold. Traditional hot sauces served with poultry include beurre blanc, velouté, mushroom, and tomato sauces, while classic cold sauces include chaudfroid, for coating elaborate dishes, and mayonnaise.

93 MAYONNAISE
Makes 1½ cups (300 ml)

Ingredients
2 egg yolks
salt and white pepper
2 tbsp white vinegar or

1 tbsp lemon juice
(more if needed)
1 tsp Dijon mustard (optional)
1¼ cups (300 ml) peanut or olive oil

1 Make sure all ingredients are at room temperature before you start. In a small bowl, beat the egg yolks until thick with a little salt and pepper, half the vinegar or lemon juice, and the mustard, if using (mustard helps the mixture emulsify).

2 Add the oil drop by drop, whisking constantly. After adding 2 tbsp of oil the mixture should be quite thick. Add the remaining oil a tablespoon at a time, or pour in a slow stream, whisking constantly. Stir in the remaining vinegar or lemon juice and season to taste.

66

94 TOMATO SAUCE
Serves 4

Ingredients
2 tbsp vegetable oil
1 small onion, chopped
1 lb (500 g) tomatoes, chopped
1 garlic clove, finely chopped
1 tbsp tomato paste
1 bouquet garni
4 oz (125 g) mushrooms, sliced

1 △ Heat half the oil in a pan and brown the onion. Add the tomatoes, garlic, paste, and bouquet garni and cook, stirring occasionally, until thick.

2 △ Remove the tomato mixture from the heat and press through a conical sieve into a bowl. Press down hard with a small ladle to extract all the tomato pulp from the mixture.

3 △ Heat the remaining oil in a small pan. Add the mushrooms and sauté until tender, without letting them brown. Stir in the sieved tomato mixture and taste for seasoning.

95 BEURRE BLANC
Boil 3 tbsp white vinegar, 3 tbsp white wine, and 2 shallots to a glaze. Add 1 tbsp heavy cream and boil again to a glaze. Remove the pan from the heat and whisk in 1 cup (250 g) diced butter. Reheat gently and strain.

96 MADEIRA SAUCE
Cook 2 garlic cloves and 2 shallots, finely chopped, in 2 tbsp butter until soft. Add 3 tbsp Madeira and boil until reduced. Add 1 tbsp heavy cream and reduce, then remove from heat and whisk in 6 tbsp (90g) diced butter.

97 MUSHROOM SAUCE
Serves 2

Ingredients
5 oz (150 g) mushrooms, sliced
4 tbsp butter
1 garlic clove, finely chopped
2 shallots, finely chopped
4 tbsp white wine
4 tbsp white vinegar
1½ tbsp Dijon mustard
1½ cups (375 ml) chicken stock
2 tbsp flour

1 Cook mushrooms in 1 tbsp butter until soft. Set aside.
2 Cook the garlic and shallots in 1 tbsp butter until soft. Add wine and vinegar and reduce to 2 tbsp. Add mustard and stock and stir to combine. Stir in mushrooms and simmer for 5 minutes.

ADD MUSHROOMS TO MUSTARD SAUCE

3 Mash the remaining butter with the flour. Whisk the paste into the sauce piece by piece until the sauce has thickened.

98 CHEESE SAUCE
Bring 1 cup (250 ml) milk to a boil. Melt 1 tbsp butter in a small pan, whisk in 1 tbsp flour and cook until foaming. Remove from the heat, cool slightly, then strain in the milk, whisking constantly. Bring back to the boil, whisking until the sauce thickens. Remove from the heat and whisk in 1 egg yolk and 4 tbsp grated Parmesan. Season to taste. Do not return to the heat or the cheese will become stringy.

99 CILANTRO SAUCE
Sauté 1 finely chopped onion in 2 tbsp oil until soft but not brown. Stir in 1 tbsp ground coriander and 1 chopped garlic clove and cook over low heat for 2–3 minutes. Purée the mixture in a food processor with 1 cup (250 ml) plain yogurt and 2 sprigs of cilantro. Return to the pan, add ½ cup (125 ml) sour cream and season. Heat the sauce, stirring constantly, but do not let it boil or it will separate. Season to taste.

68

100 PEANUT SAUCE
Serves 6

Ingredients
1½ tbsp peanut oil
6 oz (175 g) shelled, skinned
unsalted peanuts
½ onion, chopped
½ tsp dried chili flakes
2 tsp ground ginger
1 tsp brown sugar
1½ tbsp lemon juice
1½ cups (375 ml) hot water
salt and pepper

STIR NUTS TO PREVENT BURNING

1 Heat the oil in a frying pan and stir the peanuts until browned.
2 Blend in a food processor with the onion, chili, ginger, sugar, and lemon juice until very smooth.
3 Blend in enough of the hot water to make a pourable sauce. Transfer to a saucepan and bring to a boil.
4 Simmer for 2 minutes, stirring constantly to prevent the sauce scorching. Season to taste, remove from the heat, and keep warm.

101 VELOUTE
Makes 1 cup (250 ml)

Ingredients
1½ cups (375 ml) veal or chicken stock
1½ tbsp butter
3 tbsp flour
4 tbsp crème fraîche (optional)

1 Bring the stock to the boil.
2 Melt the butter in a heavy pan, whisk in the flour, and cook for 1–2 minutes until it is foaming and straw-colored.
3 Remove pan from the heat, allow to cool slightly, and whisk in the stock. Bring to a boil, whisking

SKIM FAT OFF THE STOCK

constantly until it thickens.
4 Simmer for at least 15 minutes and up to an hour, skimming if necessary. For a richer sauce, stir in the crème fraîche and simmer.

INDEX

ACKNOWLEDGMENTS

Dorling Kindersley would like to thank Hilary Bird for compiling the index, Isobel Holland for proof-reading, Pat Alburey and Fiona Wild for editorial assistance, and Mark Bracey for computer assistance.

Photography
All photographs by David Murray except for:
Jerry Young pp14–15, 16, 18, 20, 66; Philip Dowell p26;
Martin Brigdale pp34, 58–59.